RAILWAYS AROUND HAMPSHIRE

Jeremy de Souza

AMBERLEY

First published 2019

Amberley Publishing
The Hill, Stroud
Gloucestershire, GL5 4EP

www.amberley-books.com

Copyright © Jeremy de Souza, 2019

The right of Jeremy de Souza to be identified
as the Author of this work has been asserted
in accordance with the Copyright, Designs and
Patents Act 1988.

ISBN 978 1 4456 8310 2 (print)
ISBN 978 1 4456 8311 9 (ebook)

All rights reserved. No part of this book may be
reprinted or reproduced or utilised in any form
or by any electronic, mechanical or other means,
now known or hereafter invented, including
photocopying and recording, or in any information
storage or retrieval system, without the permission
in writing from the Publishers.

British Library Cataloguing in Publication Data.
A catalogue record for this book is available from
the British Library.

Origination by Amberley Publishing.
Printed in the UK.

Introduction

Since moving into Hampshire from London over ten years ago, I have been fascinated by the variety of opportunities for railway enthusiasts of any age to indulge their hobby. There's an amazing depth and cross-section of trains to see, from one of the oldest railways still running anywhere in the world to some of the latest upgrades and developments. Whatever your interest, be it steam, diesel or electric, there's something running somewhere within the county that will surely take your interest.

Railways have been a feature of Hampshire for many years. The county has key strategic routes to the capital, and is recognised as a prime commuter belt area. Cross-country routes from the south coast allow travellers to access the Midlands and beyond. The great container port at Southampton is a major freight hub, attracting container train flows from across the UK.

Historically, the region was also criss-crossed by branch lines, many of which fell victim to the infamous Beeching cuts of the 1960s. But there are still pockets of nostalgia to be found, with remnants offering historic markers (if you know where to look for them) and of course a few preserved lines.

The Isle of Wight is an ideal example of this – just a few miles off the Hampshire coast, it has long been a popular holiday destination. The sole remaining 'national' line runs for a few miles along the eastern coast, but there's also a thriving tourist line that's well worth a visit.

For younger enthusiasts, and narrow gauge fans, there are several miniature tourist lines to visit, several of which are shown in this book, all of which can be enjoyed during the popular periods.

This title is intended as a snapshot of the railways across the county, and in the space available it's impossible to show everything. I have welcomed the assistance of several photographers in the compilation of the images, and they are credited with their images. My thanks go to them for their skills and knowledge. Those photos marked 'JDS Collection' have been purchased with copyright and the original photographer is unknown.

Finally, I hope you enjoy this book and that it inspires you to explore the railways of Hampshire. Please do so safely, and never enter railway property without permission. Several of the images in this book were taken with permission and an escort at locations normally inaccessible to the public.

Jeremy de Souza
Alton, Hampshire
December 2018

Chapter 1

Basingstoke to the New Forest

Since steam days, the Down fast platform at Basingstoke has been recognisable to enthusiasts from across the country. Steam, diesel and electric trains have all posed in the afternoon sun for photos and numbers to be recorded. Wessex Electric No. 2411 catches the afternoon light before heading west towards Bournemouth and Weymouth.

Inter-regional services, now known as CrossCountry, once had decent length trains to cater for travellers. After locos and coaches were retired, HSTs provided the traction for several years. No. 43078 is seen at Basingstoke still sporting its BR InterCity livery at the head of a Virgin service.

The section of line between Basingstoke and Worting Junction is intensively used, with plenty of passenger and heavy freight services passing at all hours of the day and night. In a view compressed by the use of a telephoto lens, No. 66956 is seen powering its train of containers past Winklebury footbridge on 14 February 2009.

The flying junction at Worting, just west of Basingstoke, has been a famous photographic spot for many years, with the impressive Battledown Bridge dominating the location. At this spot, diesel services to Salisbury and Exeter diverge from the electrified lines heading towards Winchester and Southampton. This image shows a twin 5-WES Class 442 unit descending from the flyover, and re-joining the main line towards London, on 30 June 2006.

Another railtour on its way south, this time with a pair of Class 37 locos providing the motive power. Nos 37602 and 37069 are heading down past Worting Junction with The Wessexman tour of 23 May 2009, running from Crewe to Weymouth.

The flyover at Battledown offers photographers the chance of a dramatic pan shot – with No. 444045 duly obliging on a lovely sunny Saturday morning, 23 May 2009.

Micheldever station has a pleasant design, despite a sparse passenger service. There are houses and a few businesses close by, but it's hardly a booming railhead. This 2018 view shows the main building and its flint stonework construction off well in the crisp autumn light. The building is believed to have been designed by William Tite, and is Grade II listed.

Although it may not be a busy passenger station, Micheldever has a fascinating history with regard to the Second World War. When the Southern Railway was asked to assist the war effort, seventeen sidings were built and became home to an Ordnance Emergency Depot, being staffed by hundreds of soldiers. A shed over 2,000 feet long was built, and it is believed that requisitions for stores received by late afternoon were packaged and left by train that night, reaching the Normandy beaches the following day. It was also the location of a major store of oil, petrol and other lubricants. Over 18,000 gallons were stored in the tanks dug into the side of the railway cutting north of the station. The stores shed is long gone and the oil storage facility is unused, with the remaining siding being used for the storage of old wagons and the occasional stabling of maintenance trains.

Railfreight duo No. 20132 *Barrow Hill Depot* leads No. 20118 *Saltburn-by-the-Sea* past a bank of photographers at Weston with the 11.43 Burton-on-Trent to Eastleigh Depot on 7 September 2016. This was a stock positioning move in readiness for the following day's mammoth GBRf five-day tour around the country utilising all types of traction within their fleet. (Gordon White)

From Micheldever towards Winchester, the main line follows a relatively straight line, with a long loop for freight and a tunnel near Wallers Ash. This view shows No. 47812 and Wessex Electric unit No. 2416 about to enter the north portal of Wallers Ash Tunnel, running as 5T42, the 12.30 Stewarts Lane–Eastleigh Works, on 7 September 2016. (Mark Jamieson)

Recent years have seen the rise of steam-hauled dining excursions, permitting travellers to enjoy a sumptuous meal while travelling behind a famous loco. No. 35027 *Clan Line* is seen heading south from Winchester, from the footbridge at St Cross, on a special charter run on 17 January 2009.

The Weyfarer Railtour of 19 April 2008 brought the novelty of a pair of Class 20s in passenger service into the county. This versatile class of loco, dating in design back to the late 1950s, is not totally unknown in the region, with rare forays at the head of weedkilling trains in the past. Sadly, the day of this particular tour did not bring good weather, and the duo were photographed in miserable light from the public footbridge at St Cross, just south of Winchester.

On a far brighter day, No. 66720 has just passed the footbridge with its consist of engineers' wagons. The loco was painted in this livery by GBRf in 2011 following a competition held among the children of its staff.

Barely a mile further south, No. 47703 is seen heading a very short weekend charter train service. The date was 12 April 2008 and train was the Pompey Vectis Explorer from Birmingham Moor Street to Portsmouth Harbour.

No. 66517 heads north past Shawford with 4M55, the 08.55 Southampton MCT–Lawley Street Freightliner, on 29 May 2009. (Mark Jamieson)

In the days before Class 66 locomotives, the extensive Class 47 fleet was the backbone of freight operations across the UK. This image shows Railfreight No. 47209 easing its container train into the platform at Eastleigh on 23 July 1995.

The variety of routes in the south of England have always been attractive to railtour operators, and in October 2011 the Buffer Puffer tour offered participants the chance to visit many rare lines and branches. No. 37685 is seen at the rear of the charter during a brief pause at Eastleigh.

The platforms at Eastleigh station are an excellent place to watch and photograph trains, with locos stabled close by. No. 66525 is framed by the station canopy on Sunday 18 September 2015.

In the last years of the Deltics, the famous locos could be found on many special runs, taking them way off their normal east coast routes. No. 55015 is seen paused at Eastleigh during a BR-organised excursion – the Wessex Deltic tour of 17 October 1981.

Eastleigh Works celebrated its centenary in May 2009, and a major rail fair was organised, with many star attractions of visiting steam, diesel and electric motive power featuring. The event also included a 'night shoot' for photographers. No. 828 *Lord Nelson* was specially lit and made a magnificent sight for photographers.

Although curtailed early by overzealous security guards, the shoot gave the opportunity to capture many of the locos and units in unique light and surroundings. This image shows units Nos 2415, 3417 and 1497 bathed in the glow of the yard lights, during the magical blue hour after sunset.

No. 34028 *Eddystone* sits outside the main works building during the open day. This was another success story for preservation, having been rescued from Barry and returned to operational service on several preserved railways. It is currently undergoing a major overhaul and it is hoped it will return to service shortly.

No. 07007 is the Eastleigh works shunter. This class was built by Ruston & Hornsby in 1962 for BR's Southern Region. The fourteen built were primarily used at Southampton Docks, and half the class survived into preservation.

The railway works at Eastleigh has been one of the main heavy maintenance facilities on the UK railway network for many years, and is indeed enjoying a new lease of life as private operators seek skilled workmanship for repairs and refurbishment. However, for several years the depths of the yard held many treasures in the form of older diesels, left as sources of parts for their brethren. In this image taken from the Southampton Airport long stay car park, No. 58002 catches early morning sunshine. It was new into service in May 1983, and was operational until November 2000. Although currently listed as 'stored', one cannot imagine that this loco will run again.

No. 70001, the first of the class of 3,690 hp freight locomotives, heads a container train across the pointwork at Eastleigh, with just a few more miles left to go to reach Southampton. The train would have been pathed through the platform lines to permit a crew change to take place.

Class 50s were not common on the Southampton route (apart from engineering diversions), but the popularity of the class, and the number that have been preserved in operational status, means that they can be seen (and heard) on excursion trains. On Saturday 11 June 2016, Nos 50050 and 50007 have just passed through Eastleigh on the Purbeck & Bournemouth Explorer.

Passing the same location is No. 47828, hauling a charter Cruise Special. With the growth in popularity of ocean cruise departures from Southampton, it was thought that charter trains from across the UK could bring holidaymakers straight to the quay on luxurious special trains.

The Class 50s have been popular for many years, and a significant number of the Class have survived into preservation. Dedicated teams have kept several of the remaining locos in operational condition, and they continue to run on specials. Nos 50007 and 50049 are seen at the level crossing at St Denys as they leave Southampton with a return railtour from Weymouth on 8 September 2018.

A collection of liveries on display as a Virgin inter-regional HST set accelerates north from St Denys on 25 June 1999. The rear power cars and coaches are in the distinctive Virgin red livery of the day, while the leading power car is still in BR InterCity executive livery. (JDS Collection)

...he line that's still possible to this day, but the motive power and skyline have changed dramatically!
...ber 1961, Battle of Britain Class No. 34071 *601 Squadron* is seen departing from Southampton
...o was built at Brighton in April 1948, and survived in service until April 1967. (JDS Collection)

Fast forward fifty-two years to 23 April 2013 and No. 60092 has just passed through Southampton Central and is approaching the 528-yard-long Southampton Tunnel while hauling 6X44, the 12.07 Southampton Western Docks–Eastleigh East Yard. (Mark Jamieson)

Southampton Central station is also an important railway hub for the south coast, with lines from Basingstoke, Portsmouth, Poole, Weymouth and Salisbury all converging at the city. Added to this being one of the UK's main container ports, it's a popular destination for railfans. In previous years, this particular train might have been Class 33-hauled with a rake of Mark 1 coaches, but on 18 November 2018 the 09.15 Bristol Temple Meads to Portsmouth Harbour service is formed of just two coaches, operating as No. 150244.

On a bright and crisp November day, No. 158888 slows on its approach to Southampton Central with the 10.13 Salisbury to Romsey service. This unit is adorned with the latest South Western Railway livery, marking the change in ownership of the SW franchise.

As an operational unit, the Voyager Class of DMUs has put in many years of dependable service, covering most of the UK on inter regional services. Sadly, the paltry four coaches (of which one is set aside as First Class) are derided by travellers due to the limited seating capacity and resultant overcrowding. This image n 18 November 2018 shows No. 220032 making a spirited departure west from Southampton Central e 09.52 Reading to Bournemouth service.

Slowing for its station stop, BR Standard Class No. 75078 arrives at Southampton with the 08.40 Bristol Temple Meads to Portsmouth service on 7 August 1965. The loco was built in 1956 as one of eighty engines built to a standard British Railways design. It was based at Exmouth Junction and Basingstoke, eventually being withdrawn from Eastleigh shed just a year after this photo was taken. It was sold for scrap to Woodham Bros of Barry, in South Wales. Avoiding the cutter's torch, it was purchased by the Standard Four Locomotive Society and restored to working order. It can be found operational at the Keighley & Worth Valley Railway. (JDS Collection)

Diesel superpower for the fresh air express: Nos 66517 and 66956 slowly pass Millbrook, just west of Southampton, with the 06.06 Crewe Basford Hall–Southampton MCT liner train. One hopes that the return working was more heavily loaded. 10 December 2018.

There's no traffic to pick up, and just one person got off the train. No. 158882 paused at Millbrook with train 2S27, the 11.07 Romsey to Salisbury, on 10 December 2018.

Although not as popular as the Class 442s, the longer distance version of the Desiro unit is at least designed for passengers remaining on board for a couple of hours. White SWR unit No. 444004 has just passed Millbrook on 10 December 2018 with the 10.05 Waterloo to Weymouth train. It is seen passing a Freightliner service heading into the freight terminal to the left of the picture.

On summer evenings, the light is still strong enough for railway photography on the south coast. On the causeway between Redbridge and Totton, this Voyager unit catches the golden rays as it leaves Southampton behind, with Bournemouth as its destination, on 2 July 2018. (Mark Jamieson)

Another look back to the steam era shows No. 76058 on the main line near Totton on 1 April 1965. The loco was to survive another two years in service before withdrawal and scrapping. (JDS Collection)

The Marchwood branch is a remarkable link to twentieth-century history, and despite fear of closure on several occasions, it appears to face a bright future. Initially given approval in 1903, the line was built under the powers of the Light Railways Act 1896 as the Totton, Hythe & Fawley Light Railway, opening in July 1925. It was not busy at first, but later that decade the largest oil refinery in Britain opened at Fawley and traffic grew. The branch ran through Marchwood and Hythe to Fawley and served the small communities and refinery workers with steam and later diesel unit trains. Passenger services ceased in February 1966. Marchwood itself is a military port, having been built in 1943 to serve the Normandy landings the following year. It was also heavily used during the Falklands War in 1982. The last trains to the refinery ceased in 2016, but rail access to the military port remains open. The future could see passenger services return, with housing development plans making a strong case for rail access once more into Southampton. This view shows No. 37280 ambling along the branch with a single fuel tank wagon from the military sidings. (JDS Collection)

Shortly after the branch closed to passengers, the 'Hampshire Explorer' charter by the British Young Travellers Society visited the line on 21 May 1966. USA Class No. 30073 is seen running round its four-coach train, providing ample opportunity for the photographers to record the moment. The United States Army Transportation Corps built over 380 S100 Class locos for use in the Second World War. They were shipped to Great Britain in 1943 and stored awaiting the invasion of Europe. The majority went overseas but some remained in store at Newbury. As small but powerful locos were needed for shunting at Southampton Docks, fifteen were purchased and adapted for British use. Although No. 30073 is no longer with us, several members of the class have survived in preservation. (JDS Collection)

Catching the last rays of the setting sun, No. 221132 passes Sway, heading towards Brockenhurst while working 1M62, the 15.45 Bournemouth–Manchester, on 29 December 2016. (Mark Jamieson)

This photo shows a Down TC unit (NO. 414) near Beaulieu Road at the head of a Bournemouth-bound service from Waterloo. These unpowered four-coach sets were uncoupled from the REP powered units and were taken forward to Weymouth by diesel locos, typically Class 33s. The line from Bournemouth to Weymouth was electrified in 1988. (JDS Collection)

A Pullman charter no less, and the passengers had pleasant views of the New Forest from their seats on this particular day. No. 33051 is seen near Beaulieu Road on 4 July 1987 with a VSOE special. (JDS Collection)

Ashurst station, in the heart of the New Forest, was formerly named Lyndhurst Road. This image shows a semi-fast Class 442 unit passing through on a lovely summer evening while walkers enjoy the pleasant surroundings. (JDS Collection)

Beaulieu Road station lies on a straight section of line, giving plenty of warning of approaching trains. An unidentified Class 47 is seen passing with a Poole to Newcastle train on 28 May 1985. Compare the length of the train (including buffet car) to the four-car units of today. (JDS Collection)

Another view at Beaulieu Road, this time showing HST power car No. 43065 heading the northbound 'Wessex Scot' on 2 May 1992. This named service ran from Poole to Glasgow until 2002. (JDS Collection)

It is 27 June 2018 and Class 442 units are back on Hampshire rails. In preparation for a planned return to service in early 2019, test runs were held to train crew and prepare the units. This image shows a 'Wessie' ready to set off on its return to Eastleigh. (Mark Jamieson)

No. 47567 is seen deep in the New Forest at the wonderfully named location of Woodfidley with a summer Saturday inter-regional service. (JDS Collection)

The branch line from Brockenhurst to Lymington was opened initially to a temporary station in July 1858, with the permanent station opening in the town in 1860. Passengers board the branch line trains from the Down platform at Brockenhurst. In recent years it has seen a variety of traction operate these services, including the last scheduled slam-door trains on the South Western lines. This photo shows No. 159880 preparing to head off down the branch.

The section of line from Lymington Town to Lymington Pier opened in 1884, almost twenty years after the first railway ferry started running from the town to the Isle of Wight. The route is still a valuable alternative means of accessing the island for road and foot passengers. This image shows a Class 450 Desiro unit crossing the harbour bridge towards the pier station.

Typical of many pierhead stations, Lymington Pier is not grand by any means, and serves its purpose solely as a point of changing from rail to sea and vice versa. A car park adjoins the station, and a small terminal building is provided for foot and road users waiting for the ferry.

Taken from the stern of a departing Isle of Wight ferry in 2015, this overall view of the Pier station shows its layout and the associated terminal area.

Carrying The Royal Wessex nameboard, No. 34067 *Tangmere* makes light work of the 1 in 127 rising gradient as it speeds past Ashley, west of Brockenhurst, while hauling UK Railtours' 'The Dorset Coast Express' 08.44 Victoria–Weymouth on 3 September 2014. Out of sight to the rear is West Coast Railways Class 37 No. 37706. (Mark Jamieson)

Towards the end of steam on the Southern, BR Standard No. 76005 was photographed between Brockenhurst and Sway on 31 May 1966. The loco was withdrawn the following year. (JDS Collection)

Chapter 2

Farnborough to Grateley

With a dramatic curve, the South Western main sweeps through Farnborough main station and enters a long section of fairly straight four-line track towards the town of Basingstoke. Capturing a lucky patch of sun on an otherwise gloomy day, No. 159018 passes the autumnal foliage with the 09.50 London Waterloo to Salisbury on 11 November 2018.

The long avenue of mature trees continues alongside the railway for several miles west of Farnborough, and with the onset of autumn, it presents a beautiful vista to travellers. Making a steady departure from its booked stop at Fleet, No. 450034 heads east towards Waterloo with the 10.54 from Basingstoke. The new station car park provides an excellent viewing point for Up trains.

If you go down to the woods today … Not strictly on a railway line in Hampshire, but certainly within the county boundary, No. 56098 was marooned for several days at the Fleet Services on the M3 motorway after checks found that the documentation for its road transfer was not in order. The loco had been a guest at the Mid Hants Railway diesel gala of 2009. No. 56098 was one of a number of the class acquired by GB Railfreight in mid-2018 and is hoped to be seen in operation again soon.

Thrashing through Winchfield on the fast line, No. 50009 *Conquerer* heads a westbound express from Waterloo to the west. Built in March 1968, *Conquerer* saw service until January 1991 and was scrapped at Old Oak Common depot a month later.

Shortly after Winchfield, the line passes beneath the M3 motorway, and commences a long downward gradient towards Hook and Basingstoke. Passing wartime pillboxes beside the line, No. 66085 heads a freight service down the slow lines, keeping the fast lines clear for expresses. 6 April 2015.

Over recent years, preparations for the Crossrail and GW electrification programme have meant that enthusiasts could enjoy the delights of GW HSTs diverted into London Waterloo instead of Paddington. On 6 April 2015, No. 43183 glides down the bank at Potbridge with an express for the West of England.

A classic view of a Wessex Electric in its eye-catching SWT livery. 5-WES unit No. 2417 in the sun at Potbridge with a Down express.

Regular coaching stock – normally Mk 2s – must have been in short supply, as in this view a Waterloo to Salisbury service comprises two 4TC units. Being gangwayed, they would not have presented a problem to passengers, and of course the motive power that day, No. 50018 *Resolution*, would not have had any issue with the load.

No. 170306 heads past Potbridge towards London with a Salisbury to Waterloo service in January 2017. South West Trains acquired a fleet of eight two-car Class 170/3 units in 2000 (later increased to nine) to supplement its existing Class 159 fleet. All but one were transferred to First TransPennine Express at the end of 2006 in exchange for some Class 158 Express Sprinters

Celebrities before they were famous: now sporting an original HST livery decal, power car No. 43002 attracts attention wherever it goes. Although one of the earliest production HSTs, it has led a mundane life for much of its career, covering hundreds of thousands of miles. Catching the sun at Potbridge, just west of Winchfield, No. 43002 leads a diverted Up express towards Waterloo on 6 April 2015.

3 June 1967, and the end of steam operations on British Railways was nigh. Nevertheless, No. 34052 *Lord Dowding* was entrusted with the 08.35 Waterloo to Weymouth express, captured here thundering through Newnham, near Hook. The Southern said its final farewells to steam just a month later on 9 July 1967, with No. 34052 hanging on to the bitter end. (JDS Collection)

Another historic image, but this time featuring a locomotive that has escaped the cutter's torch. Photographed on a glorious summer's day in 2005, D1015 *Western Champion* heads a London-bound railtour past the elegant village of Old Basing. The loco is owned by the Diesel Traction Group, a fine band of diesel preservationists, and can still be found operating charters regularly across the UK.

Some of the fastest Waterloo–Exeter services of the diesel loco era would run nonstop from Waterloo to Basingstoke, achieving the 48 miles in well under an hour. Pausing on its journey west, No. 50017 *Royal Oak* looks superb in its colourful Network SouthEast livery, standing out against the bright blue sky. *Royal Oak* is now preserved by Boden Rail Engineering.

Hardly attracting much attention from enthusiasts, but heavily used by commuters, the Basingstoke to Reading shuttle runs from the bay platform on the northern side of Basingstoke station. On a cold and wet night on 12 January 2018, the crew of No. 165122 changes ends of the three-coach unit.

Steam on the Southern was considered taboo for many years, but thankfully main line runs are now relatively frequent. This black and white image shows A4 Pacific No. 60009 returning towards the capital, and making a steamy departure from Basingstoke on 16 August 2017.

On the Up line to London, No. 159010 makes an evening call at Basingstoke on 8 February 2018 with the 17.25 Exeter St David's to Waterloo service. The southbound Voyager alongside on Platform 4 has unusually been routed here; it is normally placed into Platform 1.

Seen from a high vantage point west of the station, No. 45669 *Galatea* departs from Basingstoke with a charter train on 9 July 2016. Although seemingly making a normal start from the station, the train stopped a few moments after this photo was taken and was then propelled back into the platform. One can only assume that perhaps a 'normal' passenger boarded the special in error!

The four-track railway continues from Basingstoke as far as Worting Junction, where the Salisbury and Southampton lines split. With less than a mile to go to the junction, No. 444001 will shortly cross over to maintain its electrified power source and continue south.

The modern steam loco *Tornado* is consistently popular and is regularly chartered for long-distance trains. Seen coming off the flyover at Worting Junction with a 'Cathedrals Express' special on Valentine's Day 2009, it is framed nicely in the low winter sunshine.

Deane, a small village west of Basingstoke, lies just before Worting Junction on the Salisbury route. Dashing past on the Up line, No. 50018 in NSE livery, with a matching rake of coaches, makes a colourful ensemble on a spring Saturday morning. No. 50018 was to be withdrawn from service in 1991, and was scrapped by MC Metals in Glasgow in 1993.

Overton is a small town, and has the nearest station to the popular Bombay Sapphire gin distillery. The station is a little way up a hill from the town centre, and has a small car park. Dashing through in December 2018 is No. 159106 with the 07.25 Exeter St David's to Waterloo express.

The Class 50s were to spend the latter years of their operational careers on the Waterloo to Exeter route, and in this photo No. 50048 *Dauntless* is seen passing from Whitchurch on a sunny morning. The station was built as part of the London & South Western Railway's expansion from Basingstoke to Salisbury, and rail services commenced in the mid-1850s. (JDS Collection)

Andover station was opened on 3 July 1854 and was previously known as Andover Junction, as it stood at the junction of the Exeter–London line and the now-defunct Midland & South Western Junction Railway running between Cheltenham, Swindon, Andover and Southampton. The current layout gives an indication that through lines once permitted nonstop services to pass through unhindered. On a gloomy day in the late 1980s, No. 207013 is seen paused at the platform with a Salisbury stopping service.

On a far sunnier day, No. 50009 *Conquerer* is seen on the Up line, ready to depart with an express to London Waterloo. (JDS Collection)

No. 50017 *Royal Oak* is seen making a departure from Andover in this late 1980s photograph. The sidings in the background are disused. (JDS Collection)

Thumping its way west from Andover towards Salisbury, and here No. 205033 makes sedate progress away from the Hampshire town. This unit, formerly numbered 1133, was withdrawn from service in December 2004 and was purchased by the Lavender Line Preservation Society in the same month. Although the centre coach was sold and is now used as a hay barn, the power cars have been restored and are in operation at the popular East Sussex line near Uckfield.

Class 50s eventually gave way to Class 47s towards the end of their working lives, with the Waterloo–Exeter run being no exception. This image shows No. 47712 (named *Lady Diana Spencer*) approaching Andover with an Up express. Later, a ScotRail blue-stripe livery was applied during overhaul at Crewe Works in early 1985, and was carried until overhaul at Doncaster in 1991. The loco survives to this day under the ownership of the Crewe Diesel Preservation Group.

How times have changed! Formerly boasting a sizeable signal box and semaphores, BR Standard No. 75066 was photographed arriving at Grateley with a mixed train of coaches and a utility van. The locomotive was scrapped in 1966. (JDS Collection)

Chapter 3

The Portsmouth Direct Line

No. 444036 passes Liss on 10 December 2018 with the 13.45 Portsmouth Harbour–London Waterloo stopping service.

In 1933 a military line known as the Longmoor Military Railway was built from Liss station to the Longmoor Military Camp. Although the railway system has closed, a few relics, such as this buffer stop alongside the current Up platform, remain as part of a walking trail.

No. 66078 passes Liss Common with the Holybourne Tanks, more officially known as 6Y32, the 08.24 Fawley–Holybourne. The train would run to Woking Yard, where the loco would run round before heading off down the Alton branch to the Holybourne terminal for the Humbly Grove inland oil field. (Gordon White)

The extension of the Longmoor Military Railway to Liss was completed in August 1933 after having to build a number of bridges and overcoming the very wet ground north of Liss Forest. The ground was so wet that the railway bed sank, the problem eventually being overcome by the laying of bracken under the rail bed.

The end of the line was fitted with a buffer stop similar to the one you can see in front of you, but shortly after its completion a train failed to stop, demolished the buffer stop and ended up over Station Road. Luckily no one was hurt but the Army decided that something more substantial was required and a concrete buffer stop was built.

In 1944 a further problem occurred when a train pushed a carriage onto the top of the concrete buffer stop. It was decided that the buffer stop needed to be made higher and it was extended to about 7 feet high (see photo). Over the years the wet had got into the concrete causing the internal steel reinforcing bars to rust and start to break the concrete structure and it was decided to demolish the concrete to ground level (see photo) and to replace with a buffer stop of the design originally installed. Tony Grant, from Liss Forest, located such a buffer stop and the Army moved it from the north of England down to Liss and is the one you can now see.

The Longmoor Military Railway Filmset

Movie makers were quick to realize what fantastic facilities the Longmoor Military Railway was able to offer. Not only were there miles of uninterrupted track running through unspoiled countryside, but they also had access to a unique collection of locomotives from across the world together with the bonus of a workforce that was able and willing to derail and rerail trains as a matter of course.

Records show that the railway was used as a location in the following films:

- 1938 **The Lady Vanishes** – starring Margaret Lockwood and Michael Redgrave.
- 1949 **The Interrupted Journey** – starring Valerie Hobson and Richard Todd.
- 1950 **The Happiest Days of your Life** – starring Alastair Sim and Margaret Rutherford.
- 1952 **Top Secret** – starring George Cole and Nadia Gray.
- 1952 **The Railway Children** – a serial for BBC Television which went out live using film made at Longmoor for realism.
- 1953 **Melba** – starring Patrice Munsel and Robert Morley.
- 1955 **Bhowani Junction** – starring Ava Gardner and Stewart Grainger.
- 1958 **The Inn of the Sixth Happiness** – starring Ingrid Bergman and Curt Jurgens.
- 1960 **Sons and Lovers** – starring Trevor Howard and Dean Stockwell.
- 1960 **Weekend with Lulu** – starring Bob Monkhouse and Leslie Philips.
- 1964 **Runaway Railway** – starring Ronnie Barker and Graham Stark.
- 1964 **Invasion Quartet** – starring Bill Travers and Spike Milligan.
- 1965 **The Great St Trinian's Train Robbery** – starring Frankie Howerd and Reg Varney.
- 1967 **The Magnificent Two** – starring Eric Morcambe and Ernie Wise.
- 1972 **The Young Winston** – starring Simon Ward and Robert Shaw.

Exploring Liss, Riverside Railway Walk

A walk leaflet for the Riverside Railway Walk is available from Chapplins Estate Agents situated on the other side of the railway crossing and is free of charge..

Information supplied by Liss Area Historical Society
www.lissareahistorical.co.uk

As well as its serious military training role, the Longmoor Military Railway was used as a location and set for several major feature films, such as *The Lady Vanishes*, *The Inn of the Sixth Happiness*, *The Great St Trinians Train Robbery*, and even *Chitty Chitty Bang Bang*. This sign by the footpath offers details and a short history.

Another view at Liss Common, this time showing No. 73138 at the head of a Network Rail test train from Portsmouth to Grove Park Depot in London on 23 November 2011. (Gordon White)

The sun glints off No. 66116 as it passes Chalton with the 08.24 Fawley–Holybourne tanks, climbing the 1 in 80 gradient towards the 485-yard Buriton Tunnel on 23 November 2011. (Mark Jamieson)

A rare sight on the railway network these days – an original and undamaged signal box. The former London & South Western Railway box at Petersfield was built *c.* 1880, and is thankfully protected as a listed building and administered by Historic England.

Although no longer in railway use, the box at the north end of Petersfield station still stands proudly beside the line. This image shows SWR's No. 444005 arriving at Petersfield with the 11.45 Waterloo–Portsmouth Harbour train on 10 December 2018.

For a while in the late 1980s, Class 50s operated some Waterloo to Portsmouth Harbour services. No. 50041 is seen at the head of a full rake of Network SouthEast coaches as it thunders south along the 'Pompey Direct' on a sunny Saturday morning.

Rowlands Castle station serves the village of the same name and was once one of three between Petersfield and Havant (the others being Havant New and Woodcroft Halt). Despite formerly having limited goods facilities, it's now a commuter station. On 10 December 2018, No. 444006 is seen arriving in the Down direction with the 12.00 Waterloo–Portsmouth Harbour service.

No. 73107 *Redhill* leads classmate No. 73138 towards Hilsea with another test train service from Eastleigh Works in December 2014. (Gordon White)

No. 73201 *Broadlands* approaches Portcreek Junction with a Network Rail test run from Eastleigh on 24 July 2012. (Gordon White)

With Portsmouth's Spinnaker Tower (built in 2005) standing proudly on the horizon, No. 73201 *Broadlands* leads 1Q05 past Portcreek Junction, heading for Eastleigh via Ludgershall, on 30 July 2014. (Gordon White)

No. 73206 *Lisa* with No. 73205 *Jeanette* on the Eastleigh–Brighton Pullman scrap train approach Hedge End on 10 February 2009. (Gordon White)

A lovely south coast vista: No. 66773 passes over Wallington Viaduct with the late-running 06.00 service from Keymer Junction on 22 October 2017. (Gordon White)

This autumn 2015 shot shows FGW unit No. 158959 at rest at Portsmouth Harbour station. The station opened in 1876 as the terminus of the Portsmouth Waterside Extension to the Portsmouth Direct Line, which runs between this station and London Waterloo. It was rebuilt in 1937 when the route was electrified, but was almost totally destroyed during the Second World War by fire after German bombing, being rebuilt after the war. It serves as an important transport hub with numerous ferries from both Gosport and the Isle of Wight linking with rail services across southern England.

Chapter 4

The Alton Line
and the Mid Hants Railway

This is definitely 'over the border' and just into Surrey, but this image is worthy of inclusion. No. 66752 is seen passing Farnham carriage sheds with the return leg of a special service to the Mid Hants Railway. In these days of sliding-door stock, it made a refreshing change to see slam-door stock on this normally mundane commuter line.

The line from Farnham to Alton is single-tracked, with the exception of a passing loop at the sleepy village of Bentley. Until 2016, the sole scheduled freight along the branch was the tri-weekly Holybourne tanks, running from the refinery at Fawley to the small loading terminal at Holybourne, just outside Alton. The oil was piped from the Humbly Grove oil field near Lasham, one of the largest inland fields in the UK. Sadly the rail services have ceased because of the alleged unwillingness of the refinery owner to upgrade the unloading equipment at Fawley, which had become life expired. The oil from Humbly Grove is now conveyed to Fawley by road. In happier days, No. 66106 is seen speeding through Bentley with the empties from Fawley. The train would run through to Alton before shunting back into the sidings.

The Holybourne tanks has produced a variety of motive power over the years. This image shows No. 60019 powering east through Bentley with a set of loaded tanks. The return working left Holybourne in the mid-evening, so this photo was only possible during the summer months.

The Mid Hants Railway has an operational connection to the national network at Alton, making it a periodic destination for excursions and locomotives attending gala events. After a spring diesel gala in 2013, Deltic No. 9009 *Alycidon* is seen hauling a convoy back to their home locations.

Daily commuter traffic to Alton is predominantly run using Class 450 Desiro electric units but there are some diagrams still using the Class 444 variants, which are better suited to longer journeys. Here, No. 444013 pauses at Bentley with a Waterloo-bound service. The Deltic-hauled light engine move was a few minutes behind this train.

On its way to Southall after a spell on the Mid Hants, No. 60019 *Bittern* and a single support coach slow for a signal check at Bentley on 3 July 2009.

The platform footbridge at Bentley is an excellent vantage point if there is anything interesting running on the branch, as seen in this view of No. 67029 heading west with the empty stock for a steam-hauled excursion on 7 June 2012. Out of sight in this view is steam loco No. 7000 *Britannia*, which would return eastward an hour or so later with the Cathedrals Express charter to Ely.

The end of the line for regular passenger services from London is the pleasant market town of Alton. With snow on the ground, No. 450029 pauses at Platform 1 before heading back towards the capital.

The line to Alton is subject to testing like any other line in the UK, but with a half-hourly passenger service throughout the day (and the single-line section), testing and monitoring specials have to operate outside the normal passenger timetable. In the dead of night on 15 October 2011, test car No. 9708 is bathed by the platform lights. The test train crew certainly appreciated the kebab van in the station car park that evening!

Another view of the Holybourne tanks, this time in the platform at Alton. No. 58031 is the train engine this time, and is about to uncouple before running round its train. No. 58031 is believed to be still in service in Spain.

Platform 3 at Alton is utilised by the Mid Hants Railway, offering an easy interchange for passengers from London. Recreating a scene from the past, Hampshire unit No. 1125 makes a fine sight (and sound) as it waits for the signal to proceed with an evening special on 3 February 2013.

The preserved and popular Hastings diesel unit has a charmed life, and from its base at St Leonards, continues to operate tours all over the UK. Traversing from the preserved line onto the national network again, the return leg of the Mid Hants Venturer begins its complex journey back to Hastings on the Kent coast on 17 July 2005.

Back in the slam-door days, 4-CIG unit No. 1302 is seen departing from Alton's Platform 1. These units were built at BREL York between 1964 and 1971, and put in many reliable years of service on Southern metals. They were eventually withdrawn in May 2005.

Platform 3 at Alton gives access to the Mid Hants Railway, as seen in this image. It's important to note that this view is not normally possible for the public – it was taken during an official 'Walk The Line' event, which is organised by the MHR each November to raise money for preservation projects.

This scene will change dramatically during 2019. Steam loco No. 925 *Cheltenham* is seen crossing the Butts Bridge interchange on the west side of the town. The smaller road arch will be replaced during the first part of the year, as part of a road improvement scheme. While the line is closed, MHR services will terminate at Four Marks.

Climbing up through Chawton Woods in bitterly cold but sunny January weather was the Mid Hants former diesel unit combo. These were sold to the Gloucester & Warwickshire Railway, but were sadly not replaced on the Hampshire line. They remain operational to this day and can still be enjoyed.

Black 5 No. 45379 puts on an incredible display of smoke as it passes through Four Marks during a photographic charter runpast. One hopes that the houses adjoining the railway didn't have any washing out to dry that day!

Just west of Four Marks, Wanders Curve presents a magnificent vista for photographers. Care should be taken by any enthusiasts visiting the area not to enter onto farmland at this point – this view, taken during an organised photo charter in October 2018, shows the magnificence of late autumn light in Hampshire and a steam locomotive working hard.

No. 34007 *Wadebridge* is currently undergoing a long-term rebuild following the expiration of its boiler certificate, but it certainly went out in style, with a magnificent series of runs on 6 March 2016. Storming up the bank from Ropley towards Four Marks, the cold morning air creates a superb display.

One of the author's all-time favourite images: this shot shows BR 9F loco No. 92212 just east of Ropley with a demonstration freight train on 6 May 2017. The spring flowers add to the classic view of the 9F working hard.

Ropley is the location of the MHR's loco shed, and the 'new' footbridge salvaged from King's Cross station provides an excellent viewpoint for train movements. 3H unit No. 1125 is seen thumping away from Ropley with a train towards Alton on 24 April 2016.

Pausing at the platform in Ropley, BR Standard tank No. 41312 simmers quietly in between turns on 5 October 2018. The BR Standard Class 2 tanks were derived from an Ivatt LMS design just after the Second World War. No. 41312 was built in 1952 at Crewe, but is recorded as having spent its entire working career on the Southern Region. This loco survived until the end of steam on the Southern, being withdrawn from service on 3 July 1967. Fully restored, the loco is a popular and regular performer on the Mid Hants.

Although steam locos dominate the operational roster, the MHR does have a few diesel locos to cater for operational needs and attract the more modern enthusiasts. No. 33202 is seen heading west from Ropley with a 'Santa Special' in December 2017, drawing the attention of a diesel fan.

Until recently this view from the lineside at Bighton Lane was unavailable due to trees and bushes. Thanks to sterling work by volunteers it has been cleared, offering this excellent view. No. 41312 passes with a special service on Saturday 5 October 2018.

On the approach to Arlesford, a public footpath beside the line gives a superb view of Down trains. BR standard No. 76017 has steam to spare as it passes on 28 December 2017. Within a couple of minutes, it will arrive at the MHR's western terminus at Arlesford.

Having led a varied life and operated across the length and breadth of the UK, No. 50027 has found a home at the Mid Hants and is a regular and popular performer. In lovely summer light, it's seen arriving at Arlesford with an afternoon service from Alton on 21 July 2013.

A truly atmospheric photo: with the last train of the day, and catching the last light of a December afternoon, No. 45379 oozes steam at Arlesford to the delight of enthusiasts on the platform.

Recreating a scene from the past, Hampshire unit No. 1125 and BR Standard Class 2 No. 41312 rest side by side at Arlesford during a photographers' charter event on 3 November 2018. A wonderfully evocative scene.

Chapter 5

Isle of Wight

There was once a petrol (and later diesel)-powered shuttle service along the pier, which opened in 1864 and closed in 1969. Although the tram cars and tracks are long gone, the supports for the trackbed can still be seen to the present day. On a foggy morning in October 2018, the rusting beams sit quietly alongside the current Pierhead station, enjoyed only by the occasional pigeon. Amazingly, there are plans to resurrect the tramway, and a new tramcar is under construction.

Although just a few miles across the Solent from Portsmouth, the small town of Ryde is the gateway to the Isle of Wight for travellers. It's sometimes forgotten, however, that islanders also commute to the mainland to work every day too. Echoing back to its days on the London Underground, 1938 stock unit No. 004 is seen at Ryde Pierhead, having just arrived on 5 October 2018. The commuters have a short walk to the waiting ferry to Portsmouth Harbour.

As late as the early 1980s, the tracks for the pier shuttle were still in place, years after the last trains ran. With the crew resplendent in their BR uniforms and caps, and with the train in full BR blue and grey livery, No. 485043 is seen at Ryde Pierhead station.

With sea mist rolling in and obliterating the view across the Solent, BR unit No. 043 rolls along the pier towards Ryde station.

Trundling slowly along the pier in March 2012, unit No. 227 is seen approaching the main town station in Ryde, formerly known as Ryde Esplanade. This is one of the island's main interchanges, offering transfers between hovercraft, train and bus services. It's also centrally placed in the town, with beaches and parks all within walking distance.

This early 1980s view shows a train of BR Class 485 stock slowing for its booked stop at Ryde Esplanade. The rail network on the island was quite extensive, and was originally operated by trains of standard gauge. The Beeching cuts saw a dramatic curtailment, resulting in the present Ryde to Shanklin line. Height restrictions in the tunnel just south of Ryde meant that only Tube-sized trains can operate, resulting in the unique operation of former London Underground units.

At the southern end of Ryde station, a footbridge provides an excellent vantage point from which to view the trains, and also the hovercraft services to and from the island. This September 2009 photo shows a two-car train departing, shortly to enter the Ryde Tunnel.

At Ryde St Johns, the island's main depot and works facility can be found. For many years the only diesel loco on the island, No. 97803, performed shunting duties and operated works trains as required. It is actually a BR Class 05 shunter (originally D2554) and was transferred to the island in 1966 to aid the electrification project. It was retained in working order and numbered No. 05001, later being transferred to the departmental fleet and numbered 97803. It remained in service until 1985, when it was withdrawn and sold to the Isle of Wight Steam Railway.

The British Rail Class 485 (4VEC) and Class 486 (3TIS) electric units were originally built for the London Electric Railway from 1923 to 1931, and were known as 'Standard' Tube stock. Bought by British Rail in 1967, they were transported to the Isle of Wight to work the newly electrified Ryde to Shanklin line. At the time of their purchase the units had already worked for over forty years on the London Underground, and thanks to the miracles of maintenance performed in the Ryde workshops, they were to provide another twenty-five years of service.

Standard stock under repair in the workshops at Ryde St Johns in the early 1980s.

A general view of the Ryde St Johns Depot showing the Standard stock cars and the diesel shunter. The introduction of electric services on the island allowed the last steam locomotives on the line to be withdrawn.

The sea air and a shortage of spares meant that several cars were broken up in order to keep the remainder of the fleet running. This driving unit, hidden from public view, was in an advanced state of disassembly.

Driving trailer No. 044 seen outside the depot at Ryde. This car survived until August 2012, when it was scrapped.

Standard VEC/TIS units passing just north of Ryde St Johns.

A lengthy Isle of Wight train heading south formed of the historic Standard stock. Most services currently have just two coaches.

No. 485041 has just arrived at Sandown station. Note the train's full Network SouthEast livery, and the signal box on the Up platform.

No. 486031 is seen heading south towards Shanklin on a sunny summer Saturday afternoon.

Another view of a full-length Standard Class unit, out in the countryside section of line near Sandown. The semaphore signal in the distance was fixed at caution, and sadly non-operational.

With the withdrawal of the Standard class units, newer Underground-sized trains were sought from the mainland, which arrived in the form of ex-LT 1938 stock. Unit No. 005 approaches journey's end at Shanklin. The last section of the journey passes industrial units and scrubland, and is not terribly attractive. The station is within the town but still a good ten to fifteen minutes' walk away from the beach.

No. 485043 at the stop blocks at Shanklin. Railways on the Isle of Wight were formerly quite extensive, and the line from here used to continue to Ventnor.

Shanklin station with a train of 1938 Tube stock ready to depart once more for Ryde. The station opened on 23 August 1864, with the buildings being extended in 1881. The structure is currently protected under Grade II listing.

The great success story for train enthusiasts on the Isle of Wight is the IOW Steam Railway. From humble beginnings at Havenstreet, it has grown to be an excellent tourist attraction. The steam line has an interchange with 'main line' services at Smallbrook Junction, and a number of combined travel packages, including the ferry or hovercraft journey from the mainland, can be purchased. This image shows 02 Class locomotive W24 *Calbourne* departing from Smallbrook Junction in October 2018 during a photographers' charter.

Recreating a scene of years gone by, *Calbourne* restarts its train from Ashey, partway from Smallbrook Junction towards Havenstreet. *Calbourne* was the first engine acquired by the embryonic Isle of Wight Steam Railway in 1967, and is the last survivor of a class that once numbered sixty. Originally built in 1891 at the Nine Elms works of the London & South Western Railway, it saw service at several depots on the mainland before being shipped to the Isle of Wight in 1925.

The Isle of Wight Steam Railway workshops are at Havenstreet, where its craftsmen carry out an outstanding programme of renovation to locomotives and rolling stock alike. By request, tours of the loco yard are given. This view shows BR Standard 2-6-2 No. 41313, and the line's Class 03 diesel shunter.

Chapter 6

Cross-County Routes

No. 207010 heads away from the photographer at Nursling in this April 1988 view. These diesel-electric multiple units were built by BR at Eastleigh in 1962 and the fleet had a lifespan of forty-two years. They were nicknamed 'Thumpers' due to the noise their engine units made. (JDS Collection)

3 December 1977 and to celebrate the end of operations with the Class 74 electro-diesels, RPPR Railtours organised a farewell run for the class. No. 74003 is seen about to reattach to the passenger stock at Romsey.

No. 59101 in full yellow ARC livery hauls a long aggregate train past West Grimstead, a few miles east of Salisbury, in the summer of 1992. (JDS Collection)

An unidentified Class 33 loco passes Dunbridge (now renamed Mottisfont & Dunbridge) with a train from Bristol heading towards the south coast on 14 May 1988. (JDS Collection)

The final batch of Class 205 diesel units, numbered 1127–33, was built in 1962 as three-car sets and intended from the outset for services in Berkshire and Hampshire. This view shows the last of the class, unit No. 1133, at West Grimstead. Later renumbered 205033, it has been preserved (as a two-car set) at the Lavender Line in East Sussex. (JDS Collection)

In very hazy light, No. 66009 passes Lockerley with a healthy load while working 6V41, the 14.47 Eastleigh East Yard–Westbury Yard daily departmental. Lockerley was the site of a huge storehouse for the US Army prior to the invasion of Europe in the Second World War, established in October 1943 and largely obsolete by October 1944, by which time supplies were being sent direct to France. The depot was just outside Dunbridge station and comprised 15 miles of sidings and 134 covered sheds. Lockerley Hall was also used to house soldiers during the First World War. (Mark Jamieson)

Chapter 7

Lost Branch Lines

Although technically 'lost', the military branch line to Luggershall, near Andover, does actually still exist at the time of writing. That said, the only trains visiting are very few and far between, and tend to be railtours. This seems to have been the case for many years, with No. 5306 seen attracting a lot of interest during a RCTS tour in 1961. (JDS Collection)

The RCTS had visited the branch a few years earlier, when, in early October 1958, 'The Sapper' tour visited with No. 30120 at the helm. (JDS Collection)

Hampshire is well known as an unofficial home to the British Army, with camps and training areas all over the county. For many years the Longmoor Military Railway was used to train the Royal Engineers in the fine arts of railway operation. It was operational from 1903 and ran between Bordon and Liss. The southern terminus had a platform adjacent to the existing main line station. This image shows LMR diesel shunter No. 878 *Basra* during an open day in October 1968. (JDS Collection)

With military personnel in attendance to warn road users, LMR loco No. 400 is seen passing the road crossing at Liss Forest on 1 May 1965. (JDS Collection)

On the same day, the loco is seen again passing through Hampshire with a special working for enthusiasts. (JDS Collection)

Probably the most famous, and possibly the largest, of the Longmoor Railway fleet was No. 600 *Gordon*. The loco survives to this day, and for many years was a regular performer on preserved lines. It is currently non-operational, but can be seen at the Severn Valley Railway. (JDS Collection)

Chapter 8

Preserved and Miniature Railways

Situated just to the south of the railway town, the Eastleigh Lakeside Railway occupies an extensive area close to a housing estate. It has an excellent running circuit and an extensive range of locomotives. The lines are laid to both 7¼-inch and 10¼-inch gauge. During the summer of 2018, the railway operated a gala event, with dozens of trains running throughout the day. This image shows a triple-header and a healthy load of passengers.

Loco No. 7 is seen in the countryside section with a shorter formation, heading back towards the main station complex. This excellent line is easy to access, and very well run – it is highly recommended!

Home loco No. 7 *Sandy River* makes a start from the central station, passing the battery-powered Eurostar replica.

The elevations of the loco are a little odd for a true Merchant Navy Class, but the two occupants of this dining special don't seem to mind too much. The short train has reached the loop at the end of the line and is about to return to the main station.

Despite the excessively dry conditions of the summer of 2018, it is understood that no fire incidents were reported at the Eastleigh Lakeside Railway. True to its name, the line is part of a modest recreational area, offering an option to those who find the steam trains too exciting. This image shows the GWR-led triple-headed train passing by.

This miniature replica of Southern loco No. 761 *Taw* was beautifully presented, and very popular at the 2018 summer gala. It was built in 1999, based on the well-known designs from the Lynton & Barnstaple Railway.

The Exbury Gardens Railway is a relatively modern creation, having been added to the beautiful grounds of Exbury House in 2001. The line is a narrow-gauge rather than miniature railway, with a 12¼-inch gauge. As with its fellow county attractions, the line offers a pleasant option on a family day out.

Partway around the circuit, the train stops briefly at a halt in the centre of the gardens. The driver offered a brief history of the line and answered questions from passengers. *Naomi* simmers beneath the trees in this view, while the driver addresses the travellers.

Back at Exbury Central, *Naomi* has just returned and the passengers can be seen leaving the platform. Exbury Garden is located deep in the Hampshire countryside, close to Beaulieu.

With the last train of the day run, *Naomi*'s driver does not need to turn the loco, and reverses onto the loop road. The railway is easily accessible and offers plenty of viewpoints for those wanting to take photographs during their visit.

The Hayling Seaside Railway operates for several miles along the coast at the popular beach area near Portsmouth. Although looking like a steam loco, No. 3 is a diesel replica.

Loco No. 12 *Jack* crosses an open crossing as it makes its way westwards back along the coast between Eastoke Corner and Beachlands. The line opened in 2003 and remains popular with holidaymakers in the sandy coastal area of Hampshire.

One of the most unusual lines in the county, and reputedly the oldest working pier railway in the world, is at Hythe. From the quiet village, the railway runs 700 yards along the Hythe Pier, connecting with a ferry to Southampton.

Threatened with closure many times, the railway still ekes out a living saving regular travellers a long walk along the pier, and of course as an attraction to enthusiasts. The locos have a unique history. They were built by Brush as battery locos for use in a factory in Avonmouth making mustard gas in the First World War. With the war over, they initially saw industrial use before bring converted to third rail electric propulsion.

No. 2 is seen setting off along the pier in this January 2014 view. The pier itself is well over 100 years old, and both it and the railway are listed as items of significant historical interest.

Another view of one of the locomotives, this time in 1988, when both loco and coaches sported an attractive blue and white livery. (JDS Collection)